Table of Contents

Introduction 2
Before Reading This Handbook 4
My Biggest Challenge 5
20 Reasons Why Your Sound System Sucks! 6
Best Practices 7
Mixers 9
The Room 16
Controlling The Sound 17
Amps/Amplifiers 19
Speakers and Monitors 20
Cables and Connectors 25
Microphones 28
Input 31
Drums 33
Sound Room vs Control Room 35
Additional Equipment 36
The Best Audio Set Up 40
Recording the Service 44
Sound Check (the bad word!) 45
Safety 46
Sound Check Checklist 47
Church Sound Ministry Quiz 48
How do you get started? 51
List Your Current Equipment 52
List Equipment Needed 53
Quiz Answers 55
Index of Figures 56
Draw a diagram of your church sound system 58

Introduction

We often say we want to give God our best. We say that we want to give more to the church than we give to the world. Oh really? If this is true, then why is the church sound equipment old, worn, outdated, and neglected? Drums are usually treated with the most disrespect. Cymbals are cracked, worn, or old. Pianos are never in tune. Keyboard and Organs have dirty, broken, or worn keys. Cables are missing or damaged. Speakers are blown or not connected properly. Mixers have no unified EQ for each identical channel. Mics are a mismatch and most are not color marked at both the mic and the mixer. Nothing is properly labeled and the cables are not neat and professional. However, I have also visited churches where they did respect their sound and video equipment and everything was in order. How your sound system looks may make positive or negative impressions on visitors and your congregation.

> *"If faith comes by hearing, shouldn't our church sound systems be a priority? Many churches invest heavily in audio and media systems, and others, unfortunately, do not. Whether you're a small, mid-size, or mega-church, church sound systems that will allow the Word and the music to be heard with detail at the appropriate level for your congregation, based on the style, culture, and make-up of your church, should be one of your highest priorities." (source: Sharefaith.com)*

What is the solution? There are several approaches to designing or redesigning a sound system. You can have a large budget and spare no expense to purchasing high-quality, high-end professional equipment that will make your service sound professional. You can also settle for less and purchase the cheapest equipment and suffer the consequences of unwanted noise, interference, equipment failing, and equipment unable to upgrade due to incompatibility with older equipment. I'm not implying that old equipment is bad or unusable. Often the older equipment depending on what it is works better or just as good as newer equipment.

> *"Old Isn't Necessarily Bad... Old doesn't mean unusable. Think of all the people who trashed their tube amplifiers for solid-state stereos thirty years ago, only to find audiophiles preferring the warm sound of tube amps later. So, take the time to examine your gear. Does it work? Is it worth repairing? Can it be repurposed? Is there another ministry that can use it?" (source: blog.shure.com)*

The first important questions to consider when designing or upgrading your sound system are what exactly do you want? What is your budget? And what equipment do you currently have? Many people don't know what they want. It's important to have an idea of what you want to be satisfied with the results. You need to either design a system according to what you want and your budget. By not knowing what you want you may make purchases that you don't need. You will waste more money in the long run by not researching and knowing how the equipment will ultimately be connected.

There are several options when it comes to connecting equipment. If you don't know what you want or plan out your project you may find that you wasted time, money, and energy on equipment that was incompatible or outdated. The easiest installations to design are new installations. You can purchase new equipment which will have new cables, wires, and connectors. Over time cables, wires and connectors wear and begin to lose the ability to conduct electricity which produces a "clean sound." Another installation that requires more planning and time to apply is large budgeted, high-quality installations. Large, budgeted installations allow a church to customize a unique sound system. These installations can include wall or ceiling mounting for speakers, digital mixers, video or projection monitors, sound monitors, and ceiling microphones. Running snakes through walls or ceilings. Purchasing high-quality high-end digital equipment. A large budget allows for designing mixing consoles and building sound rooms to hold all of the key components of your sound system. The majority of the churches may already have some sound equipment in place. This equipment can include a basic P.A. system, speakers, wires, mics, etc. How this equipment is set up can improve or cause the system not to run optimally. Church leaders may not know how to properly set up or take advantage of the equipment already in place. Mixers and P.A. systems may be wired incorrectly, proper settings on the mixer may be overlooked, and equipment may need repair, replacing, or reconfigured. With a church that may already have equipment in place. The only option is to upgrade or swap out old or damaged equipment. The last option is to not upgrade or make any additional purchases. This option involves taking advantage of any existing equipment currently in place. There may be no budget for purchasing additional equipment. You have to use the equipment that you already have. In this option you may need to configure your equipment to work to its optimal performance. It is a true saying concerning sound systems "You get what you pay for." There are some things in this world that you can get away with buying or settling for the least expensive.

> "You get what you pay for. If it sounds too good to be true, it probably is. You've heard those old sayings before, but they're true. Good equipment costs money. Don't buy anything (cords, cables, mics, speakers, mixing boards, really anything in your system) just because the price is low. Buy it because you know it will work well and reliably. Talk to colleagues at other churches, read publications designed exclusively for church and production technology, attend seminars and workshops, and build a relationship with a trusted AV provider." (source: Blog.shure.com)

How can this book help you? I am NOT a salesman. I do not sell equipment. I provide a service. This service includes making your sound system work to its peak performance. Purchasing professional, quality and reliable equipment will yield a professional quality and pleasing sound. Your sound system should be an investment. A good system should last several years.

My experience with making cheap purchases is a story concerning the tires on my motorcycle. Motorcycles are dangerous vehicles by themselves. It is imperative that you use quality parts when riding 70 to 80 miles an hour on the freeways. I was strapped for cash but I needed to replace my tires. My mechanic put on the cheapest tires that he had. The conclusion of the story ended with me having bubbles in my tires. They did not last long and could have caused me to have an accident or worse. Since that close call, I have never placed cheap tires on my motorcycle again. The moral of my story is to purchase the "best quality" sound equipment if you expect it to sound good, be dependable, and last.

Is the sound department treated as a ministry? Why would you neglect a ministry if it enhances the service? Why have a great church building, a powerful pastor, new carpet, comfortable seats, nice bathrooms, a professional pulpit, and other awesome amenities but your sound equipment looks and sounds horrible? That doesn't make any sense to me. You are not investing in the audio ministry because you feel it's not a ministry. The audio ministry is important because it involves not only providing praise and worship to the congregation and to the ministers it is also essential to how the message is amplified and distributed throughout your church. Your sound equipment reflects your entire ministry. What good is having a great choir if the congregation can't hear them clearly? What good is having a dynamic, powerful, and spirit filled preacher if the congregation can't hear their message clearly?

Before Reading This Handbook

Before reading this handbook, please note I am not a sound expert! I have no audio engineering degree or audio certification. My experience is through building and maintaining recording studios and live equipment my entire life. I am not an English major and I may have made English and grammatical errors in this book. Every topic listed in this handbook can be researched and studied through magazines, books, or using online resources. I am not trying to re-invent the wheel. What I have done in this handbook is combine all of the topics and equipment that is needed to either design, upgrade or maintain a church audio system. You may already have a person who may have designed and maintains your sound system. However, this person may have limited knowledge on how to fix, optimize or improve the current system you are using. My job is not to prove how inadequate your system may be. My job is to open your eyes and minds to the possibilities of **improving** your current sound system. The goal is to also **optimize** what equipment you may already have in place. My pleasure is also to help you make informed choices before upgrading your system. This handbook is not a "sound system bible." This is not a "how-to" book. This handbook does not teach you how to run a sound system. However, it can be used as a guide to help you understand the many components concerning a complete church sound system. My expertise is from experience setting up, maintaining, and running church sound systems. The heart of my ministry is focused on consulting and design. I DO NOT know everything about audio systems. I use the wisdom that God gave me and the experience to provide you with excellence. God deserves our best but we lack this element when it concerns the church sound system.

My Biggest Challenge

My biggest challenge will be trying to teach an old dog new tricks. That may sound harsh but it's true. I have experience working with pastors who may have had experience running DJ or sound systems in the past. 20 or 30 years in the past. The technology of sound equipment has changed. I know that some of the sound equipment in some churches has been in the church since the church has started. Over time equipment and cables fail. My biggest challenge will be convincing pastors and those over the purchasing of new equipment to upgrade, update and modernize their equipment. It can be as simple and inexpensive as replacing your cables and changing out your connectors. Pastors who tend to think they know what's best for musicians tend to resist change. E.g., If I feel that the drummer (I am also a drummer) needs a monitor, the pastor may not agree with my suggestion. Even though the drummer is complaining that they can't hear the music or the vocals behind the drum cage. Even though the drummer knows that they need a monitor and my initial assessment points to this fact, the decision and the purchase depend on the pastor. The best scenario that I have encountered is where a pastor allows me to freely re-design the system without objections and intervention. I know that some pastors will try to avoid spending more money on equipment that they may "need." My job as a consultant is to identify issues with a sound system and only make suggestions and recommendations to improve it. The challenge is also getting pastors to upgrade their systems and integrate new technology such as computers, digital mixers, high-end professional cables, etc. I am not a salesman I provide a service, the choice of equipment is solely based on the pastor's budget, taste wants and needs. The most important thing to think about when upgrading or optimizing a sound system is what will be good for the "people." I've witnessed a lot of pastors catering the sound system around their comfort and their taste without considering the experience of the "people." I would recommend and suggest that any purchase, improvement, or upgrade be centered and focused on pleasing the intended audience. You get what you pay for when it comes to music equipment. My job will always be centered on giving God my BEST and ministering to the people. The goal is not to buy the cheapest equipment I can find at a pawn shop. However, oftentimes you may find occasional deals at pawn shops. I will never suggest purchasing used equipment. If you can afford to buy new equipment do it. I am not into cutting corners because God does not cut corners with us.

20 Reasons Why Your Sound System Sucks!

1. You have no dedicated person to run the sound system.
2. Your mixer or P.A. system has no or limited busses or auxiliary outs.
3. You have no monitors for playback.
4. Your volume and EQ settings are causing feedback.
5. You are using cheap cables.
6. You're not using XLR cables for connections.
7. You're not using a digital mixer.
8. Your speakers are in the wrong location.
9. You have old, outdated, or damaged equipment.
10. Your mixer does not have enough channels.
11. Your amp does not have enough Wattage.
12. You are using old cables and connectors.
13. Your sound equipment is not centralized.
14. The drums are too loud. – You need a drum cage.
15. Unable to use new technology such as iPhones, Tablets, cellphones, etc.
16. You are using cheap microphones.
17. You are using the wrong type of microphones.
18. You are using speaker wire for speakers.
19. Unable to set/change wireless channels on mics.
20. You are not using re-chargeable batteries for mics.

Best Practices

1. Don't mix and match models. (all mics, amps or speakers are different)
2. Try to match brands. (e.g., Yamaha amp, Yamaha speakers etc.)
3. Make a diagram of all equipment.
4. Inventory all equipment. (model names and numbers)
5. Know what type of connections and cables you will use.
6. Replace cables frequently. Over time cable quality decreases (interference)
7. Use only professional connectors such as XLR, Speakon and ¼" or better.
8. Lubricate mixer and all electronic connectors. (Fader lube)
9. Conduct sound checks before service.
10. Keep voice and music playback separate if possible. (distortion)
11. Keep the musician's playback volume and the FOH mix separate. (using monitors and mixer busses)
12. Use rechargeable batteries. (save money)
13. Label all cables, mixer channels, and speakers /monitors with tape.
14. Avoid: Distortion, interference, feedback, grounding, crosstalk, drop-outs, and noisy signals.
15. Know what type of mics you are using. (directional mics, dynamic mics)
16. Try different audio designs. (You are not stuck with one configuration) All sanctuaries are different. Design what's best for you.
17. Check your EQ. start in the middle (from 1-10 start at 5)
18. Keep your audio cables separate from power cables. (Cross talk)
19. Purchase wireless receivers with multiple/auto selecting channels.
20. Don't strain your cables. Don't place objects on top of cables. Don't pull your cables. (cables are delicate)
21. Keep your un-used mixer channels on mute – to reduce noise and hiss

22. Make sure your electricity is grounded properly.

Mixers

What is an Audio Mixer?

An audio mixer allows you to direct and send audio signals to desired area/zones. There are several types of mixers to choose from. There are analog mixers, digital mixers, powered mixers, P.A. Systems, consoles, all-in-one mixers which includes amp, mixer and speaker. A mixer allows you to collect and centralize all input sources including music, vocals, instruments etc. and create a pleasing "mix" for an audience or congregation.

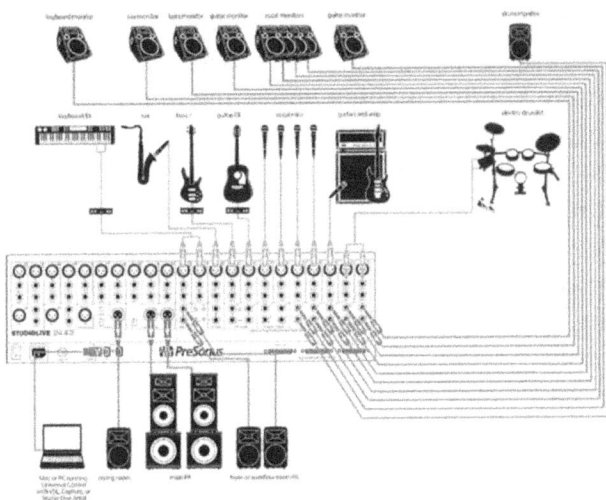

Figure 1 - Mixer Setup

Analog mixers – A combination of knobs and faders that allow you to control the volume and tone of audio signals. Analog mixers are normally easy to operate. An Intuitive process of signal flow. If you compare an analog mixer and a digital mixer. An analog mixer is like using a normal wired telephone inside of your house. A digital mixer would be like the cell phone or cordless.

The pros and cons of using an analog mixer can vary depending on who you ask. An analog mixer is just that... analog not digital. The sound quality is not going to be as clean or clear as a digital mixer. Sometimes this is a desired effect. You may want a warmer more natural sound. Analog mixers cannot remember your settings from one set/service to the next. You will have to individually label and mark each channel settings including fader and knob positions. This could be daunting if you have a lot of channels like a 24 channel or more mixer. A digital mixer can remember settings (called programs) and return the mixer to a default setting or a programmed setting. Analog mixers tend to be bulkier and require more space due to components and power supply. While digital mixers are smaller and take up less electricity.

Figure 2 - Analog Mixer

Digital mixers – Digital mixers work like analog mixers but uses digital signal processing technology. Digital mixers can save and recall the positions of faders and knobs. This can be useful if your church has different services that require different set up needs. This can also be helpful if you have many hands touching your mixer and some settings may be changed by mistake. Using a digital mixer you can save "programs" to recall or reset your mixer back to the way you wanted. E.g., If you're normal sound person is not available to work the mixer for a special service. Most people who lack experience with a mixer will try to push every button, raise, and lower every fader and turn every knob until they hear the desired sound. The pros and cons of using a digital mixer may also vary depending on who you ask. By using a digital mixer you can recall the desired settings by simply recalling the saved program. Digital mixers are usually smaller and compact compared to analog mixers. Another benefit of using a digital mixer is that is allows you to have more channels to use without compromising space. A negative of having a digital mixer is learning how to use and program the mixer. Often digital mixers can be controlled using an application on a computer or smartphone.

Side Note: These settings should NOT change from one service to another. Once you have "peaked out" the optimal level for each mic (which should all be identical) you don't need to touch the settings. All you need to do is turn on the mixer and amp, place batteries in the mics and if they are wireless and turn on the wireless receivers if you have them… The point is you don't need to have custom settings for each mic.

The choir may have 4 different singers and for some odd reason you will change the EQ and volume for each mic to adjust to each choir member…. This works well if you are recording the vocals. From my experience with sound systems and from visiting numerous churches. There is never a dedicated person to run the mixer. Therefore, all of the mic levels and EQ should be either identical (if the mics are identical) or each mic should be "matched" so there is no need to worry if one mic is lower in volume or EQ than any given mic. A digital mixer can recall the "default" or desired settings. Meaning if the choir is about to sing, you have programmed your digital mix for that performance. You can set a "program" just for the choir. Once the choir has finished you can re-set or put the mic levels and EQ back to another defaulted program. This is how professionals run live performances. But sense most churches do not have dedicated sound ministry, no one would know how to run a digital mixer even if the church had one. Having a digital mixer is like having a sports car but you don't know how to get it out of 1st gear, It's useless. If you can figure out how to program the digital mixer then it is a very powerful tool that can alleviate many issues within the sound system of the church.

Figure 3 - Digital Mixer

Figure 4 – Rack Mountable Digital Mixer With Software

Powered Mixers - Powered mixers are analog mixers with built-in amplifiers. Most churches use this type of mixer/amp to amplify both microphones and instruments. Power mixers can connect directly to speakers. These types of mixers are often portable.

Figure 5 - Powered Mixer

P.A. Systems – P.A. Systems is an all-in-one set up that includes a power mixer, speakers and speaker cables. These are usually light weight and best used for small events. If you have a mid to large size sanctuary a P.A. System may not be adequate. This is especially true if you continue to upgrade your music ministry. If you have many instruments, a large choir, and several floor mics. You may have outgrown your P.A. system and don't know it. You may need to upgrade your P.A. system to include a 16 channel or more mixer or console with aux outs or busses.

Figure 6 - Typical P.A. System

What is a console? – A console is usually a recording term used to describe a mixer that resides inside a recording studio. A console has typically 32+ channels and would cost several thousands of dollars. Both terms mixer and console can be used interchangeably. The most commonly used term in churches or live performances is mixer.

Figure 7 - Mixing Console

Channels – Although there are differences between analog and digital mixers. All mixers have at least one channel. A channel allows you to connect a sound device such as a microphone, instrument, CD player etc. to the mixer. Mixers come in different sizes and styles. The function of the mixer also varies. What a mixer does is allow you to send audio signals where you want and need them. The use of busses, auxiliary outs, sends, subs and sometimes called "groups" and any other term that means the same thing. These functions can be used to further control your audio signals. Some mixers are 8 channels, 16 channels, 24 channels and up. If you have a very large church you may need a 24 and up channel mixer to control your service. If you have a small church you may be able to get away with a mixer that will mainly use microphones. The size of the mixer will vary depending on your need and expansion. I personally feel that most churches can get away with a 16-channel mixer in most cases. However, having more channels allows you more function and flexibility for growth. Having many channels is not the primary advantage of a mixer. ***Having control over each channel is what this entire handbook is focused on***. In the next section <u>Controlling The Sound,</u> it focuses on distributing sound from each channel to a specific location or area in the room. Channels allow you to control audio input and then send that audio signal to another device such as a monitor amp.

Auxiliary/Sub/Bus/Send (Splitting The Sound) – Stand-alone mixers are not amplified. You must have an amplifier in order to hear the audio signal. In the case of a typical mixer, whatever sounds that come from each channel is then sent to an amp. Each channel is balanced meaning it uses 2 channels left and right. By moving the balance knob to the left you will only be using the left side of a given channel. By turning the knob to the right, you will be using the right side of the channel. By keeping the balance knob centered you are now using both sides of one channel. If you are using a 2-channel amp one side of the amp corresponds to the mixers left and right channels.

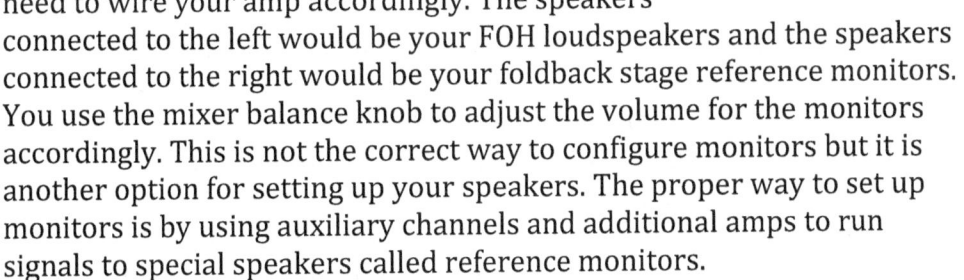

A cheat for using loudspeakers and monitors is by using the left side of your amp for your loudspeakers and you can use the right side for monitors. This would mean you need to wire your amp accordingly. The speakers connected to the left would be your FOH loudspeakers and the speakers connected to the right would be your foldback stage reference monitors. You use the mixer balance knob to adjust the volume for the monitors accordingly. This is not the correct way to configure monitors but it is another option for setting up your speakers. The proper way to set up monitors is by using auxiliary channels and additional amps to run signals to special speakers called reference monitors.

The use of "sub channels" can further help control audio signals. Each mixer manufacturer may call this function something different. The variations can be called Busses, Auxiliary Outs, Sends, Subs, Groups, or a combination. Such as Aux Out, Aux Send, Sub Out etc. If your mixer name has a number it will tell you the function of that mixer. E.g., If your mixer is a mixer with 8 channels and no Auxiliary outs it will simply state 8 channels in the name of that mixer. If a mixer have sub outs, aux out and send it may state in the name of the mixer that it's an 8x4. Which means it has 8 channels and it has 4 busses. Other variations include 12x4, 12x8, 16x8, 24x4, 24x8, 48x8 and so on.

Figure 8 - Mackie 24x8 8-Bus Series Mixing Console

I have two different mixers with these types of channels. One mixer calls it "auxiliary out" or aux out and another mixer calls it "sub out." They both do the same thing. They both allow one channel to be split by re-routing or re-assigning the signal into "sub" channels. For example, if you have a 12-channel mixer with 8 sub channels. These sub channels may be called Auxiliary out, Send, bus or Subs. This will allow the FOH engineer to distribute audio signals to specific areas such as stage monitors, effects, recording devices etc.

Figure 9 - Mixer with Auxiliary Outs

The more auxiliary outs that you have the more monitors you can support. The key is to have the same amount of aux channels, amp channels and stage monitors. If you have 4 zones or areas that needs monitors. You will need a mixer that has 4 or more Aux outs, you will also need 4 amp channels (either two 2 channel amps or one 4 channel amp) and you will need 4 passive or active monitors. Having a regular 4 – 16 channel mixer with no auxiliary, subs, sends or busses your mixer will not be able to support multiple monitors. I carefully stated multiple monitors because many smaller mixers will support only one monitor.

Figure 10 - A 4 channel (non-auxiliary) mixers I own

This type of mixer will not allow me to control multiple monitors on each of the 4 channels. However, you can control one loudspeaker and one monitor by splitting two channels and using the main out Left and Right respectfully. The Left channel can go to the main P.A. System and the Right can go to one monitor. This is not how this mixer was designed but you can route the channels to fit your unique application. Also, what I've noticed on P.A. systems commonly used by many churches I've visited. In the back of the mixer it already has ONE monitor function. You will be able to control a playback monitor which includes ALL channels. The main purpose of Auxiliary outs is to control the signal for each individual channel.

Figure 11 - Mixer Aux Channels

Input Channels – Input channels are channels that is used to connect a microphone, CD player or other audio device. A Mixer has several channels. Each channel has its own unique inputs. The input types may vary from XLR, RCA, Speakon or ¼" etc.

EQ (Equalizer) – Many P.A. Systems and Mixers have built in EQ's. An EQ allows you to control the overall tone of the signal. The frequency can range from lows, mids to highs. It is best practice to keep the EQ settings in the middle/center or flat. The problem with many churches is multiple EQ configurations. The mixer may have an EQ, the P.A. System may have an EQ, the powered speakers may have an EQ and the individual amps may have its own EQ. That's 5 EQ's! With that many EQ's working at once you can over process a signal. The purpose of amplifying a signal is to increase the signal without losing the quality of the signal. The more you amplify, EQ, send a signal you reduce the quality of the signal with each process you put the signal through. Basically, if you're using older or cheap equipment the signal quality will be loss.

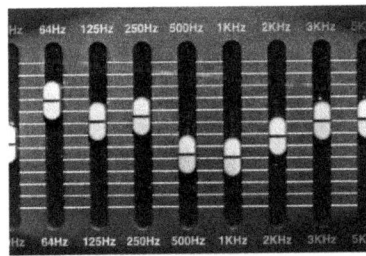

Figure 12 - EQ

VU Meter vs L.E.D. Light – A VU meter stands for volume unit meter or standard volume indicator (SVI). A Meter Bridge allows you to view the strength of a signal on a mixer. A meter bridge can either be analog (a needle) or it can be L.E.D. (Light Emitting Diode) lights.

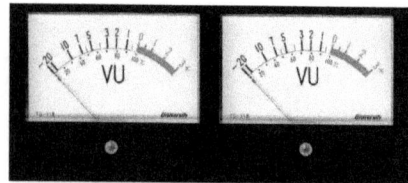

Figure 13 - VU Meter

My Experience: One of the issues with using small or cheaper mixers is the inability to view the strength of the signal for individual channels. Most small mixers do not have a VU meter or meter bridge. If a vocalist or someone is talking normally you will not be able to know which channel the vocalist is using. Marking both the microphone and mixer channel may not always be the solution. If someone is holding the mic and covering up the colored tape then the use of color coding is useless. If someone who is not trained would try to work the mixer they would not automatically know that the color on the mixer channel and the color on the wireless mic means. The safe way to know which channel is being used is by using mixers equipped with VU meters for each channel. Most of the smaller mixers I have seen only use a L.E.D. or needle VU meter for the main output and not for individual channels.

Preferred Brands: Alesis, Allen & Heath, Avid, Behringer, Carvin, Cerwin-Vega, Gemini, Mackie, M-Audio, Nady, Peavey, PreSonus, Roland, Soundcraft, Yamaha

The Room

Figure 14 - Sanctuary

The Environment – The bottom line about the environment is the acoustics of the room. This includes the walls, windows, floors, seats, ceilings, carpeting, padded chairs etc. All of these things make a difference on how sound is absorbed. Acoustic treatments can help tune the room. There are different approaches for tuning or treating a room. The use of absorbers, foam, diffusers, sound barriers, construction materials, isolation platforms etc. can improve the overall sound quality.

> *"The physics of the propagation of sound is immensely complicated, and when the assortment of materials that make up the walls, floors, and ceiling (plus any windows, doors, and furniture) are added to the equation, it's very difficult to predict what will happen to sound waves once they've left their source. What's more, every room is different, and it's not just the dimensions that will dictate how the room will sound... Imagine two rooms of the same shape and size. One has two-meter-thick concrete walls, and the other a single-layer plasterboard stud-wall. Even with those brief,*

albeit extreme descriptions, you probably know already that the two rooms will sound very different. Add in the multitude of room shapes, sizes, wall - construction methods and surfaces found in home studios, and it becomes impossible to provide a one-size-fits-all guide to acoustic treatment." (source: Soundonsound.com)

(The Propagation of sound. Sound is a sequence of waves of pressure which propagates through compressible media such as air or water. Sound can propagate through solids as well, but there are additional modes of propagation. During their propagation, waves can be reflected, refracted, or attenuated by the medium.)

Figure 15 - Acoustical Wall Panels to absorb sound

Controlling The Sound

By using busses, sends, subs, and aux outs you can control the sound in each area in your church. This may be a difficult concept to understand and it is very challenging to explain in words. Sense there are 4 interchangeable words that are used for the same exact function. I will refer to these functions as busses. The best way to explain the use and purpose of a bus is to allow each area or zones to have its own unique mix of sounds. For example,

let's say we have a 12x8. Which is a 12 channel by 8 bus mixer. It is very wise to draw a diagram of your church to identify each area that needs audio. In this example we will have 6 areas/zones. Each church will vary depending on size and the needs of the church. The largest complaints in church sound systems are that the drums are too loud, no one can hear the choir, or the keyboardist is too loud. Although there are several quick fix solutions to resolve those examples. You can ask the drummer to play lighter (good luck with that). You can install a drum cage/shield, you can install a drum room, you can mic the choir etc. Although these are great solutions, the lack of space and a smaller budget may prevent those choices. The professional solution may also be costly depending on how much equipment you have already in place. The solution is to realize that every area needs its own monitor. I discuss more about Speakers and Monitors later. The list of areas that would need a monitor can include (not in any specific order): choir stand, pulpit, organist, drummer, guitars, keyboards. Each area/zone should have its own monitor (speaker). By using busses, you can send a specific signal to any of the desired areas. The drummer may say that they cannot hear the keyboard when they play. This is an easy fix when using a mixer using busses along with an amp and monitor for EACH area. Meaning if you have 6 areas/zones you will need 6 channels for each monitor. Notice I didn't say you needed 6 amps. Keep in mind each stereo amp has 2 channels. Which are channels left and right. Which is 2 channels. If you can afford to have 3 amps you would have 6 channels (2 x 3 = 6). But there are more efficient methods by using multi-channel amps discussed in the <u>Amps</u> section.

Using channel #1 for the keyboard you can use bus #1 which has its own knob on channel #1. Buy labeling each bus and each monitor you will be able to distribute the keyboard signal (on channel #1) to any of the available busses/monitors in the room. We will also call the monitor placed next to the drummer as monitor (you guessed it #1). You have channel #1 which is your keyboard channel, on the knobs of the keyboard channel you will find knobs labeled as bus which are usually numbered bus 1, bus 2, bus 3 etc. Usually located on the bottom right-hand area of each mixer will be your bus channels. Don't get those bus channels mixed up with your normal input channels. An individual amp needs to be connected to the output for bus #1. The point is to have your drummer and keyboard player present for a sound check. As the

drummer and the keyboardist begin to play. The drummer will tell the mixing engineer who is located at the FOH (Front of House) to turn up or down the volume of the keyboard (on bus#1). The Mixing Engineer will use channel #1 (which is the keyboard channel), then they will find the knob labeled as bus #1. The use of the bus channel allows the volume to be controlled across all mixer channels. The drummer will either signal to turn the volume up or down as desired. Although this monitor may be heard at different areas or zones, each zone should have its own unique monitor. The EQ'ing of a monitor may vary but it is usually a neutral signal which is flat. The purpose of the monitor is not to give more highs or low frequencies. The purpose of a reference monitor is just that, it's a reference of the signal which will allow a musician to hear the proper playback in real-time. Audio signals bounces off of walls and objects. This is called "Reflection of Sound." Depending on how large the church is the signal may bounce or delay by the time the sound reaches the other side of the room. Sound waves react differently depending on what surface it hits. By having a monitor it allows the drummer to hear the keyboardist in real-time. To sum up this section "Controlling The Sound" you must realize that "Centralized Control" its accomplished by 3 elements:

- A mixer that has busses.
- Amps with independent ins and outs.
- Monitors in each area you want to distribute an audio signal.

As mentioned before, the name of the feature may vary from busses, aux out, sends, or subs. The function of these "sub" channels is to further control the audio signal to where you want or need them. This is the professional set up for live performances. In ministry it is not a performance or entertainment but the audio set up is identical for live performances and stage venues.

"The bottom line: good sound is good sound. A church building is a performance space, so all the usual rules of sound reinforcement apply." (source: Blog.sure.com)

Amps/Amplifiers

Figure 16 - 4 Channel Amplifier

Amplifiers – An amp is an electronic device that can increase the power of a signal. An amp can be a separate piece of equipment or it can be contained within another device. Amplifiers may have various input and output connectors such as XLR, ¼" instrument connector, Speakon connector and so on. Without an amplifier you will not be able to hear a voice in a large room. Instruments rely on amps to increase the volume of the sound. There are different types of amplifiers depending on its use. Guitarists use guitar amps which are tuned especially for the high and mid ranges for a guitar. Bass players use bass amps which provide lower frequencies best for bass guitars. Keyboard players can use normal amps but also have specialized amps and speakers just for keyboards. Drums needs to be mic'ed for amplification which allows you to control the volume of the drums. Some churches may use electronic drums sets. Organs have built-in amps which works in conjunction with a Leslie or external speaker. An organ will also need to be Mic'ed and the mixer FOH will control the playback from the organ to the audience. Amplifiers are essential to a service or live show. Amps are rated by Watts, channels, and RMS (root means square). Amps comes in different sizes and configurations. It is usually a square device with several knobs in the front to control the volume. Located in the back of the amp are input and output sockets. A professional amp will come with a built-in fan. Cooling is a main concern for any instrument that stays on for any extended time. An amplifier can heat up and in many cases cut off to protect its circuits. Older amps have fuses that can be blown if the amp gets too hot. You must choose a well-ventilated area to house your amp. Some amps may also be loud while running due to the fan. The location of an amp varies depending on space and location. You can use rack mounted amps to save space.

Amp Channels - Amps also can have one, two, four or more channels. Most audio amplifiers come in two channels. These channels are usually in stereo which is left (one) and right (two). The opposite of a stereo amplifier would be a mono amplifier. Another use for a mono channel would be for an instrument such as a microphone, guitar, bass etc. The instruments that would need a stereo connection would be a keyboard which sounds better using both the left and right channels. Other professional amplifiers can have more than two channels. A 4-channel mixer can be used when powering monitors on stage/pulpit. By using 2 4 channel amps you have the ability to power 8 monitors (2 x 4= 8).

P.A. Systems (public address) – A P.A. System is an all-in-one system that includes a mixer, an amp, 2 speakers and cables. A P.A. system is primarily used for voice but also can be used to amplify music.

Figure 17 - P.A. System

My Experience: Amps need to be cooled and depending on the model the amp can be noisy. Amps need to be placed in an area that will prevent interference with wireless microphones. I have experienced amps cutting off in the middle of service due to it overheating. I simply removed the fuse (which did not blow). I waited a few minutes and restarted the amp and it began to work properly again. I've also have blown amps by not allowing the amp to breathe (cool) properly.

Preferred Brands: QSC, Marshall, Peavey, Behringer, Yamaha, Fender, EV, JBL, Bose, Line 6, Pyle, Crate, Roland, Markbass, Crown

Speakers and Monitors

What is a speaker vs a monitor?

The term speaker and monitor are often used interchangeably. But they are two different types of sound equipment. A speaker (which is also used to describe a person who is talking) is usually amplified and powered. A stage monitor or monitor is usually a non-powered cabinet that is used on stage facing the performer. Each monitor needs its own amplifier if it is a passive monitor. An active monitor has a built-in amplifier and it requires electricity to work. Another reason for using passive monitors on a stage is to reduce the number of cables and wires. This prevents a tripping hazard and electromagnetic interference when laying audio cables next to power cables. Since many words are used interchangeably I hope you now understand the difference from a loudspeaker vs. a reference monitor. A loudspeaker can produce a sound for both audio and voice. A reference monitor can produce sound for both audio and voice but is EQ'd only to give you a "reference" of the desired voice or instrument. A loudspeaker may include high's, mids and low frequencies so you can hear the sound clearly. A reference monitor may only give you mids and some lows. The on-stage monitor is not to be used to be pleasing to the ear. It is used to ensure a vocalist can either hear themselves, other vocalists or the desired instrument when performing a song. Musicians will use a stage monitor the same way. The musician may desire to only hear their own instrument out of their personal monitor or they may want to only hear the vocals as they play. By using monitors and the correct mixer a musician or vocalist/minister can customize their individual playback volume. Without using monitors for any reasonable sized church will hinder the musicians and the vocalist's ability to hear themselves or others. This can result to a poor vocal performance.

Figure 18 - Loud Speaker

Speaker or Loudspeaker – The technical term for speaker is an electroacoustic transducer which converts an audio signal into sound. Speaker types include full-range, Subwoofer, mid-range, and tweeters.

Monitors – Different types of monitors include studio monitors, stage monitors and in-ear monitors. Studio monitors are used inside of a recording studio for audio production and engineering. In-ear monitors are used by performers on stage or in a studio. Stage monitors are usually in a cabinet that is (wedge-shaped) to face the performer or speaker.

Figure 19 - On Stage Monitor

A normal speaker cabinet is square shaped. With a monitor the physical speaker, tweeters or horn is facing up or in an angle to allow the performer to hear the playback clearly. Stage monitors are used for performers on a live stage. By using stage monitors the FOH engineer is able to distribute playback to any performer or area that needs to hear a specific instrument or vocal. This is the core of upgrading a typical P.A. system into a professional live stage environment. The use of monitors is essential in order to distribute specific sound to specific areas of your church, stage, or room. Another technical term for stage monitor is called a foldback. The sound engineer point of view is called the FOH (front of house). The performer's point of view is called performer-facing. Which means the speaker, pastor or minister, musician or choirs is facing the audience or congregation. Monitors are usually full-range frequencies. Meaning they are not designed to give your more highs over mids or lows. They are used to give you a "reference" of the desired sound you want to hear. Some studio monitors are also called reference monitors. Stage Monitors are either active or passive. Active monitors have a built-in amplifier and can be plugged directly into the mixer. The downside to active monitors is that you have to power the monitor. Passive monitors do not have built-in amplifiers. They do not need power to carry a signal. For each monitor you will need one channel from an amplifier. E.g., If you have a 2 channels left and right (stereo) mixer you can power 2 monitors. There are different approaches for setting up monitors. Monitors can be controlled by the central FOH mixer or they can be controlled by a separate on-stage mixer. Often monitors can be controlled by performers on-stage. This set up would require an additional mixer/amp set up on-stage. Most churches only use a P.A. type system running both vocals, choir, music, and the speaker through one mixer, one amp and two Left and Right (stereo) speakers. In order to equalize/distribute the sound to the desired areas. By using a mixer with (busses, aux out, sub outs or sends) or using two mixers, one for the main FOH system and the other just for the monitors. The problem with allowing musicians or vocalist on-stage to control their own playback is that they may increase the volume too high for the FOH system. The purpose of monitors is to reduce the need to increase the playback volume and allow the FOH engineer to set the playback for the audience. This is why FOH speakers are facing the audience while Monitors are facing the performer.

> *"In most mid- to large-size venues, there is a separate sound engineer and mixing console on or beside the stage creating a mix for the monitor system. The monitor mix is often different from the "front of house" mix because performers may request to hear more of certain accompaniment or rhythm section instruments. In the most sophisticated and expensive monitor set-ups, each onstage performer can ask the sound engineer for a separate monitor mix for separate monitors. For example, the lead singer can ask to hear mostly her/his voice in the monitor in front of her/him and the guitarist can ask to hear mostly the bassist and drummer in her/his monitor." (source: Wikipedia.org)*

Stage monitors allow the FOH to give each performer or area its own unique, specific mix of any instrument that is fed through the mixer. This is why it is very important to purchase or upgrade to a mixer that has Busses, Aux out, Sends or Sub Outs. A small 4 to 8 channel mixer my not have this capability. Even a 24-channel mixer may only have 4 Busses or none at all. Having many channels don't help because you can't control the use of monitors without auxiliary outs for each channel. Without a foldback system or monitors the on-stage side would hear the reverberated reflections bouncing from the rear wall of the room. This causes a delay and the sound is distorted. This will often cause the singer to sing out of time with the band. I millisecond delay can cause the drummer to be out of time with the keyboard/piano or organist. Another function of using a monitor is to provide performers a dry mix. This mix is absent of reverb, echo, delay this will also help the performers to stay in time with the other vocalist or musicians.

I spent allot of time on monitors because I feel that mixers with auxiliary or busses, amps with independent channel inputs and outputs along with passive or active monitors is mandatory to control the sound in any venue. You can also use monitors to send audio to other areas outside of the main sanctuary. You can have monitors in ceilings, overflow rooms, hallways, bathrooms, pastor's office, exterior locations, and other common areas. Monitors help you control the overall level of multiple areas. To summarize monitors is to point out that if your mixer does not have aux outs you will not be able to control multiple monitors.

Figure 20 - Ceiling Monitor

Headphones – An alternative for using monitors is to use wired or wireless headphones. Headphones allow musicians to hear their own desired playback without increasing the volume on-stage or the FOH volume. One of the biggest issues I've noticed with churches is the musicians playing loud through their on-stage amp or P.A. system. This also increases the FOH volume which can drown out other performers such as vocalists or other musicians. Many professional churches and live venues use headphones for playback.

In-Ear Monitors - High-end venues may use in-ear-style headphone monitors. These units may be one size fits all or can be a custom mold specific to the performer's own ear. This is typically done by an audiologist.

Wireless speakers – Are easy to understand. The drawback with wireless or Bluetooth speakers are maintaining power. You can use a wireless speaker system that uses rechargeable batteries. Those batteries will need to be replaced or charged for each service.

Figure 21 - Wireless Speaker System

On-stage musician amps – Sometimes instruments are connected directly to the FOH mixer only using DI boxes. Guitar players, Bass players, and often keyboard players may use their on-stage amplifier which is designed specifically for their instrument. Often these amps are not adequate to fill in a larger church, venue, or room. When this happens, a musician may crank up the volume and distort their sound by trying to push their amp or P.A. system past its limits. This causes louder uncomfortable volume for other musicians, performers, vocalists and often the audience themselves. To resolve this issue the musician can use their amp or P.A. system for their playback. They can "send" an audio signal from each amp or P.A. system back to the FOH mixer using DI boxes. That will allow the FOH engineer to include the instrument with the FOH mix. It is NOT the job of the musician to decide or determine the FOH mix. Unless the musician is also responsible for the FOH, the musician should only be concerned with their playback volume. Many musicians think that louder is better. In professional recording or live performances, a cleaner signal is better. The conflict arises when the musician is also responsible for the FOH mix. In this scenario, the musician may mix their instrument louder than other musicians and vocalists intentionally or unintentionally. The best practice is to focus on three systems. The P.A. system should only include pulpit speakers, choir, and anything using microphones, larger loudspeakers should be used for instruments and musicians, and monitors should be used by each musician to improve FOH mixes. It is not recommended to use the P.A. system for both pulpit speaking/vocalist and for playing music out of the same speakers. This normally causes distortion. In the churches that use organs, the organ can be mic'ed. This will allow the organist to set the Leslie as a monitor for themselves for playback and the FOH can set the volume for the audience using the FOH mixer. Another purpose for mic'ing each instrument including the organ is for recording the service professionally. If your keyboard player does not want to connect their instrument or amp to the house they will not be recorded. Recording the service is another important reason why you want to connect all instruments to the FOH mixer. This is also centralized control where the FOH mixer can mix exactly what will be recorded on tape, CD, or video.

Figure 22 - Guitar Amp

Figure 23 - Bass Amp

Headsets – There are different types of headsets that have several uses. In television, headsets are used to communicate to stage and camera crew. The control room would communicate with each crew member via headset. Headsets can either be listen-only or they can also have microphones to communicate back to the control room. The headset can be wired or wireless. Headset sizes can range from large sound blocking sets to an earpiece that can be custom fit for each member just like the in-ear monitors. Headsets can be used to communicate with other musicians to give sound information such as key changes, order of songs, special instructions, etc.

Figure 24 – Headset

My Experience: The elements that ensure an equal, clean, and professional sound includes mixers with auxiliary outputs, amps with independent ins and outs, and the use of powered or passive monitors. I have witnessed both types of setups. Churches with monitors and those without. I found that the churches that don't use monitors suffer from the most sound-related issues. Issues include music being too loud, mic feedback, and musicians unable to hear other musicians or vocalists. Every environment will require a special and unique setup. Not all church sizes will warrant using monitors. The biggest sign that you may need to use monitors is if you find complaints about not being able to hear other vocalists or musicians. If your choir does not have monitors you are doing a big disservice to them.

Preferred Brands: Peavey, Behringer, Mackie, Gemini, EV, Yamaha, QSC, Roland, Yamaha, American Audio, Presonus, Alesis, Pioneer, JBL, Bose, Audio-Technica, Carvin, Cerwin-Vega, Crate, Fender, Korg, Pyle

Cables and Connectors

Cables – Two or more wires running side by side and bonded, twisted or braided together to a single connection. Cables are used to carry electric currents. Cables have shielding and insulation. The insulation does not prevent electrical interference. The cable shielding protects and prevents electrical interference. It's either braided or foil. Cheap cables provide less insulation, which increases interference (noise).

XLR cables – An XLR cable is primarily used as a professional mic cable. Older microphone cables used ¼" Phone Jacks. A professional microphone has a connector that looks like a round 3 whole connector. The XLR cable is not just used for microphone cables. If you notice the back or top of professional mixers you will find two types of XLR connections. You may find the female end of the XLR connection on each channel. The master volume out connections are usually XLR connections.

Figure 25 - XLR

¼" Phone connector – Phone jacks are connectors that are located on each channel of the mixer. Another name for ¼" connectors is instrument cables. From my experience mixers comes with at least two types of input connections XLR and ¼" Phone Jack. If you are still using RCA connectors which are usually phono jacks, you need to throw it in the trash immediately. RCA may still be used in rare situations when using a tape or

CD player to record the audio. RCA connections are still commonly used in car audio systems.

3.5 Mini phone connector - 3.5mm Phone jacks are smaller than the ¼" jacks and is primarily used for headphones and other smaller devices like cellphones, laptops, and audio PC connections. Phone cables comes in mono, stereo, and tip/ring. The mono cables have one stripe at the tip, stereo cables have two stripes and the tip/ring connector has three stripes.

Figure 26 - 2x ¼" Male and 1x Female (mono)

Figure 27 - 3.5mm Mini Phone Connector

Speakon – A speakon connector is a professional connector mainly used for loudspeakers and amplifiers. Speakon cables allow more currents to flow between devices. They have a unique design that prevents air or electric shock over XLR and ¼" jacks. They also lock into sockets with a twisting motion. They are identified by a round male and female socket. The connectors are usually blue.

Figure 28 - Speakon connector

RCA cables (Radio Corporation of America) – This connector is sometimes called a phono connector or A/V Jacks (Audio/Video). These cables are usually identified by red and white connector. For composite video there will also be a yellow connector. An RCA connector is typically and older type of connector used for components such as record players, tape decks, and car audio etc.

Figure 29 - RCA

Stage Box – Another name for this device is called Cable Snake Box or Audio Snakes. This is a multi-cable device that allows instruments to be connected to the mixer. The stage/pulpit can connect devices to long runs of cable that connects the mixer or FOH. These devices have a square box that allows you to connect microphones or other instruments. It uses either XLR or Instrument Jack connectors or a combination of the two called a combo connector. A combo connector allows you to either plug an XLR or a ¼' instrument jack. Having a combo connector gives you more flexibility when connecting equipment from and to the FOH mixer.

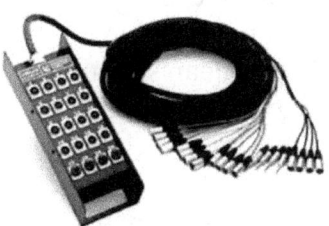

Figure 30 - Snake Box

Other Connectors - There are other types of connectors such as Optical, Banana, TOSLINK and so on.

Patch Cables – Patch cables can have a shorter length because it's primarily used for equipment that is closely located to each other. Can be less than a few inches in length.

Attenuation – Attenuation is the reduction of audio signal (electrical current) that is reduced over a long run of cable. Higher quality cables reduce or prevents attenuation that may occur with a long cable or by connecting too many cables together. E.g., If you try to connect a speaker using speaker wire and you find that you are not getting a signal, most likely is due to the cable being too thin and not allowing enough current to flow over a long distance. Cable size is measure by gauge. The smaller the gauge e.g., 0-gauge means that the cable is thicker than a 4-gauge cable or wire. The larger the cable or wire the more current can pass through the wires.

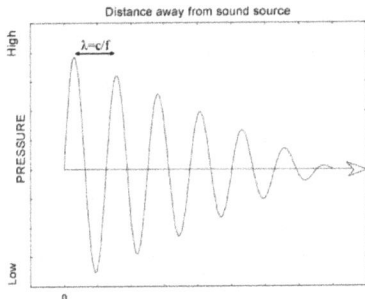

Figure 31 - Attenuation

Repeater – *A repeater is an electronic device that receives a signal and retransmits it. Repeaters are used to extend transmissions so that the signal can cover longer distances or be received on the other side of an obstruction.*

Figure 32 - Audio Repeater

My Experience: Over the years I have collected cables and connectors. I keep a box filled with cables that I collect and store. You never know when you will need a specific cable or connector. Cables and connectors are not cheap. I have purchased devices from The Guitar Center, Radio Shack, Best Buy, and other audio and video stores. Often I will buy a device and it will include cables or connectors that I do not need at the time. I simply save those cables and or connectors for future use. You get what you pay for. The free cables are usually not high quality but yet those free cables are useful when needed. The cables are rated on how well they carry the signal. The insulation and the material used for the connectors are very important to produce a clean signal. As mentioned cables are also rated by the gauge or thickness of the wires carrying the signals. Gold-plated connectors tend to send a cleaner signal.

Preferred Brands: Belkin, Audio-Technica, Behringer, Boss, Fender, Line 6, Livewire, Monster Cable, Nady, Musician's Gear

Microphones

Microphone (mic or mike) – A microphone is a transducer that converts sound into an electrical signal. The commonly used microphones are dynamic, condenser, and piezoelectric microphones. There are other types of microphones such as valve microphone which uses a vacuum tube. Microphones are typically connected to a preamp or preamplifier before the signal can be recorded or reproduced. There are different types of condenser microphones such as RF condenser, valve, and electret microphone (electret was not a typo). Condenser microphones are considered higher-end microphones. These are the type of microphones you may find in a high-end professional recording studio. Electret microphones are used in most common applications such as cellphones, computers, PDAs, and headset microphones. Dynamic microphones are robust and most commonly used on stage. They provide less feedback than other types of microphones. Some microphones require phantom power to operate due to their construction. If you plug in a microphone directly to a mixer and you hear no sound. It could probably be due to it needing phantom power. Most mixers may have a button to turn on phantom power. If your mics need phantom power they may not be suitable for live performances.

Figure 33 - Dynamic Microphone

Direction – Microphones are not one size, one shape or one pattern fits all type of instrument. There are several designs based on the directionality of the sound waves that enters the mic. These types include omnidirectional, unidirectional, bi-directional, cardioid, shotgun, etc.

I have an AKG Perception 200 cardioid-pattern, large-diaphragm, true capacitor microphone. It has a low-cut filter and a -10db pad. The type of microphone that I have would primarily be used for professional studio recording. The cardioid microphone is named because the pattern is "heart-shaped". Cardioid microphones are commonly used for live vocals due to the cardioid response reducing pickup from the side and rear, helping to avoid feedback from the monitors. This type of mic requires phantom power to operate. **The importance of knowing what type of microphone you have will determine how that microphone should be used or held**. A vocalist who holds a unidirectional mic away from their mic may not get a good signal due to the design of the microphone. Microphone types vary from speaking mics, vocal recording mics, instrument mics, drum mics, stage mics, lavalier mics, etc. All mics are not designed for every scenario. There are also hyper-cardioid microphones such as a shotgun microphone. This type of microphone is commonly used on television and film sets.

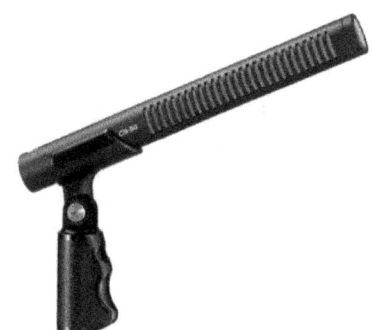

Figure 34 - Shotgun Microphone

A Lavalier microphone is designed for hands-free operation. These smaller microphones are worn on the body. They are more often fastened to clothing with a clip, pin, tape, or magnet.

Connectors – The most common connectors are Male XLR, ¼" phone connector, 3.5mm, USB, etc.

Figure 35 - XLR

"The 3-pin XLR connector has two advantages over a 1/4" connector. It provides balanced audio, which means that the cable is protected against electrical interferences from mobile phones or other devices. The longer the cable the more this can be an issue if you don't use XLR cables. An XLR cable can transport 48 V phantom power that some microphones need. Of course, your mixer must be able to supply this phantom power." (source: Wikipedia.org)

Wireless Microphone - A wireless microphone contains a radio transmitter that needs to send the signal to a wireless radio receiver. The transmitter and receiver may also use infrared waves within sight of each other. A wireless microphone is also known as a radio microphone. There are many different technologies for transmitting audio signals such as using UHF or VHF frequencies, FM, AM, or other digital modulations such as digital and Bluetooth. There are many advantages to using wireless microphones which include greater freedom of movement for artists or speakers. Cabling problems such as moving and stressing the cables. Reduction of trip hazards on pulpit or stage. The disadvantages are reduction in working range. XLR microphones can run up to 300 ft. or 100 meters without suffering from attenuation. Higher-end wireless microphone units may transmit at a longer range. Interference with other radio equipment or other radio microphones. You should get models with many frequencies synthesized selectable channels. Operation time is limited relative to battery life. Noise and dead spots can occur. You are limited in the number of operating microphones at the same time and place due to the limited number of radio channels (frequencies).

> *"Every wireless microphone system transmits and receives sound on a specific radio frequency, known as the operating frequency. The crucial element in using wireless systems is the right choice of this operating frequency. You cannot combine arbitrary RF frequencies as the microphones will compete with each other, and each system will experience noisy interference and/ or dropouts."* – (source: Shure.eu)

Figure 36 - Wireless Microphone System

Figure 37 - Cheap mic using a phono jack

A special note about microphones: if you notice the microphone has a ¼" or instrument connection or it has an on/off switch most likely it is not a professional mic. Although the use of the on/off switch is useful most professional mics do not have that function. It has been my experience that using mics with on/off switch over time the switch will eventually fail and no longer allow you to turn the mic on or off.

Batteries / Rechargeable - Use rechargeable batteries for each service. Always have more than enough batteries for devices. This will allow you to recharge batteries while still powering other devices. The problem with rechargeable batteries is that they do not recharge themselves. Someone needs to collect the rechargeable from devices, place them on the charger and reinstall them in the devices before the next service.

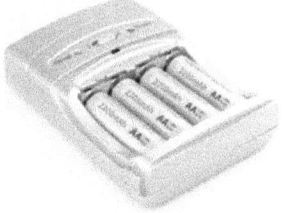

Figure 38 - Rechargeable Batteries

Stands – Dome-shaped round metal base, folding tripod base, boom arm. I prefer folding tripod (3 leg) stands. They offer more support for weight and allow you to maneuver and place mics in better positions over the dome-shaped round base mic stands.

Figure 39 - Typical Microphone Stand

My Experience: I have used several types and brands of mics over the years. I've found that not all mics work the same. You need to know what the mic will be used for. Studio mics are not stage mics and mics that you would use on a live or acoustic instrument may not work well with voice. You need to understand how a mic works. You can have uni-directional mics, dynamic mics, or mics that will pick up in all 360°. The point is not all mics work the same. You need to know how the mic will be used before making purchases. Cheap mics using cheap cables will produce a cheap sound. If you mix and match microphones you will need to use various volume and EQ settings to compensate and match the sound. In a rare situation, I encountered a wireless system with identical mics but all of the mics had a different EQ and volume even with using the same receiver. This situation was rare and I had to adjust each channel to match the EQ and volume. If you have 4 mics that are identical and all are using the same receiver all mics should have the same settings on your mixer.

Preferred Brands: Nady, AKG, Line 6, M-Audio, Peavey, Sennheiser, Shure, Sony, Behringer, Audio-Technica, Rode

Input

Input Socket – There are a few common input sockets located on each channel's pathway. The most common are XLR, ¼" Jack, and RCA. Input sockets on higher-end and more modern mixers include Optical, FireWire, Speakon, USB, S/PDIF, and BNC.

Figure 40 - Rear of Mixer

Input Devices – Mixers allow you to mix both audio and vocals together. Along with audio and vocals, a mixer allows input from other devices. Including CD players, laptops, cell phones, PCs and other audio and video equipment.

Figure 41 - CD player

My Experience: Using CD players for playback during a live service is always risky. The issue is not always with the quality of the CD itself. CDs are prone to scratch! So, if you playback the CD during a performance it will either skip or stop playing altogether. The CD may not always be the culprit. CD players need maintenance. You can go for years without cleaning the CD player laser. However, cleaning the laser can greatly improve the sound quality and playback of an audio CD. Although homemade CDs may work on most CD players some CD players are unable to play non-professional-made CDs. The issue with a live church service is that most people don't treat the house of God professionally. In a professional live stage performance, there will be sound checks. These sound checks will allow the sound mixer to cue and inspect the quality of a CD or other playback device like an iPod, Ipad, laptop, cellphone, etc. Most church performers will only approach the sound engineer right before they are to perform. By using a combination of both an internet source, CD, and MP3 you may already have the song that will be performed on your computer connected to your mixer. By using a digital file, you prevent the issue of a scratched CD. The downside of MP3s is that you may not have the exact version of the song and you have to have a fast processor to playback the file on the fly. A PC needs to have internet access and be able to stream music quickly. You can then use Youtube or any other online music source to playback the exact song that the performance requires. This all depends on if you are given advanced notice. Using cellphones, iPods, ipads, etc. are not always wise because of three main factors. The battery may die in the middle of the performance if it is not connected to a power source, The 3.5mm audio connector may not be compatible with the 3.5mm connection you are using for your mixer auxiliary inputs, and cellphones and Ipads may have alerts, messages, alarms, and notifications that can interfere with the performance. Another issue with using cellphones and ipads is the use of passwords. Every few minutes the password may be required and the screen will time out. The owner will need to keep putting in the password to play the song. Another issue with using cell phones or tablets during a church service is unexpected calls, alerts, and system sounds. The easiest method is to have the performer give you the song before the service. You extract the audio from the CD or by using a thumb drive. You play the Mp3 or Wave file directly from the church PC directly into the church mixer for playback. In other words, **try** not using a CD player as much as possible to playback music during a live service. If not, you're asking for playback trouble.

Drums

Drums are a vital and commonly used acoustic instrument in most churches regardless of denomination. Although vital the sound that the drum produces can cause havoc to your overall sound level. Drums are loud and depending on the size of the church building the sound can overpower both listeners and other musicians. There are several approaches to prevent drums from causing an issue. While placing the drummer in the back is not always the solution. The position of the drums does play a role in how you can control the overall volume of other instruments. Another common issue with drums is the snare. If you are rehearsing or performing a song without drums the drums are prone to rattle or vibrate causing an annoying vibrating sound. This is caused by deep or bass frequencies vibrating the "snare" on the bottom of a snare drum. This can be prevented by simply switching the "snare" level off.

Drum Cage / Drum Shield – A drum cage/shield is a structure that is either portable or stationary that either prevents sound from a specific area or contains sound for recording purposes. Some cages are made with plexiglass, plastic, or other material. Some drum cages are actual small rooms built specifically for drums. These rooms are sometimes equipped with drum mics and headphones for playback.

Figure 42 - Typical Drum Cage

Figure 43 - Drum Room

Mic'ing Drums – The reason you would mic drums is not just to hear the drums louder. An alternative reason for mic'ing the drums is for recording purposes. Think about it, if you connect a recording device to the FOH mixer what will be recorded? The mics will be recorded and any other instrument that is connected to the mixer will be recorded. However, the drums will not be clearly heard because they are not normally mic'ed. You can hear the drums bleeding into mics but that is not professional. To have a proper recording each instrument should have a FOH mix. This mix can include drums, choir, keyboard, guitar, bass any other instruments, and also whoever is talking through the P.A. system.

Don't Blame The Drummer – I am also a drummer. I understand how some may blame the drummer for the overall volume of the music. This is true in some cases where the drummer does not understand dynamics. *Relative loudness. The two basic dynamic indications in music are: p or piano, meaning "soft". f or forte, meaning "loud".* If the drummer has only two volumes loud and louder this forces all other musicians to compensate. This increases the overall volume on the stage. Louder is NOT better. The best sound is low and clear vs. loud and distorted. The drummer can contribute to the tempo, feel, and volume of the band. To improve the playback concerning the drummer you can place a monitor near the drummer. The FOH can give the drummer the special mix that they desire. E.g., You can give the drummer more drum playback volume, or you can give the drummer more bass guitar mix or more vocals. This will drastically reduce the need for the drummer to play loud if they can hear their playback or if they can hear the desired instrument to help them keep perfect timing. Some of the audio problems can be resolved by the drummer learning how to play softer to match the current environment. Using sound cages and drum room can eliminate the need to force the drummer to play softer or lower. I have recently heard of a device that can help a drummer be in touch with their low end. It's a drum seat amplifier. Many drummers can't feel their bottom end or bass, this can be due to simply using cheap drums, bad acoustics, muffling the kick drum, etc. By using a drum seat amplifier, the drummer can feel their low end and will reduce the need to amplify the kick by using a mic.

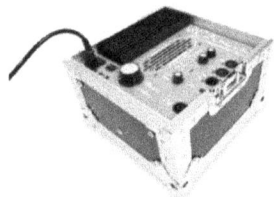

Figure 44 - Drum Seat Amplifier

Preferred Brands: There are no special brands when it comes to drum cages. What you are looking for is stiff Plexiglas that will not bend. You want the 4 panels to be able to support themselves. Buying a cheap version of a drum cage made from plastic or a flexible material will cause the cage to bend. You want to find a cage/shield that will allow you to run cables underneath without touching the cables. You want a thick cage but still be able to see through clearly.

Sound Room vs Control Room

The purpose of this booklet was to also emphasize the importance of centralized control and centralized cabling. Not every church has the space, resources, or budget to afford an isolated room for a mixer, amps, and other sound equipment. My experience with church sound systems revealed that many churches place their P.A. systems, amps, wireless receivers, etc. within the podium itself or on the pulpit. This is a bad idea for several reasons. Many pastors wear many hats inside of a smaller church. The pastor may also run the sound system and preach during a service. If there needs to be an adjustment in the middle of the service and the pastor is not near the mixer. Who can go onto the pulpit and make the adjustment? If the mixer is in a position or location that only the clergy has access to, then those in the clergy should know how to properly run the equipment. Many of the churches that I've visited regardless of size did have a dedicated room to run a mixer and other audio equipment. Running cables from a sound room to a stage or podium is not very expensive if you use the "correct" tools. Having a centralized place to control the sound allows a person FOH to adjust any mic, speaker, monitor, etc. These rooms have several names such as control room, sound room, etc. If the mixer is surrounded by walls or it is located in the front, side, or back of the church. Having a centralized area or room to control the sound is essential in a professional environment. If your church has a sound room all of the cables running from the monitors and loudspeakers should run to the mixer and amps in that room. The best location to control the sound is to place the mixer at the rear and center of the stage, room, or sanctuary. This location is called the FOH or Front of House. Everyone wants great sounds from their system but not everyone wants to invest money in their church. Having a sound room may require more work, effort, and budget but in the long run, it will improve the service by centralizing the sound of the service. Another issue with sound rooms is not using reference monitors inside of the sound room. Another purpose of having a FOH mixer is to mix all of the sounds using a mixer. A sound room should have some small reference monitors that will allow an engineer to mix all of the collected sounds for the audience. If the sound room does not have a reference monitor the engineer must "guess" the appropriate playback. Often the sound room or mixing console is not centered in the rear of the room. Having an offset location for mixing creates an uneven playback sound for the FOH.

My Experience: Having a control room has its advantages over an open roomed FOH mixer. A control room allows you to run all of the cables to a centralized location. You can securely store valuable equipment such as sound and video gear inside a closed room. A closed FOH room can also be useful to avoid sound technician conversations interrupting the service or event. A sound room can provide more than just privacy, security, and centralized cable management. A sound room can store unused "sound" equipment, keep unwanted hands off of valuable gear and it can also provide a space to get a true mix. Often churches use the sound room as an extra junk storage room or as an extra closet. I worked with one church sound room. The first thing that I did was clean out the sound room. I removed anything that did not have to do with the sound system. I got rid of old, unused, and broken cables. I got rid of the spider webs, and trash and used dead batteries. Within a few days of cleaning out this room, I found more trash and non-sound equipment inside the room. This causes a problem if you need to access sound equipment but can reach it because there is trash or junk that is obstructing your access. Something to think about.

Additional Equipment

Compressor – *A signal processing operation that reduces the volume of loud sounds or amplifies quiet sounds by narrowing or compressing an audio signal's dynamic range. (source: Wikipedia.org)*

Figure 45 - Compressor

Noise Gate (Expander) – *"A noise gate or gate is an electronic device or software that is used to control the volume of an audio signal. Expanders are generally used to make quiet sounds even quieter by reducing the level of an audio signal that falls below a set threshold level. A noise gate is a type of expander." (source: Wikipedia.org)*

Figure 46 - Noise Gate

Limiter – *"A limiter is a compressor with a high ratio and, generally, a fast attack time." (source: Wikipedia.org)*

Figure 47 - Limiter

Equalizer – *"Equalization is the process of adjusting the balance between frequency components within an electronic signal." (source: Wikipedia.org)*

Figure 48 - Equalizer

Rack Cabinet – *"A 19-inch rack is a standardized frame or enclosure for mounting multiple electronic equipment modules." (source: Wikipedia.org)*

Figure 49 - Cabinet

Power Strips and Surge Protectors – *"A power strip is a block of electrical outlets that distribute AC power to electrical devices such as computers, audio/video equipment, appliances, power tools, and lighting. (source: Tripplite.com) A surge protector is an appliance or device designed to protect electrical devices from voltage spikes." (source: Wikipedia.org)*

Power strips and surge protectors are not the same. Power strips allows you to connect multiple devices. The power strip does not provide any protection for devices. A surge protector attempts to limit the voltage supplied to an electric device by either blocking or shorting to ground any unwanted voltages above a safe threshold.

> *"Many power strips have basic surge protection built-in; these are typically clearly labeled as such. However, power strips that do not provide surge protection are sometimes erroneously referred to as "surge protectors"." (source: Wikipedia.org)*

Figure 50 - Power Strip

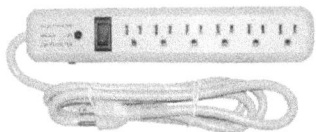

Figure 51 - Surge Protector

Power conditioners – *"A power conditioner functions as a voltage regulator and line conditioner to adjust under - and over voltages, maintaining smooth 120V nominal output. Because optimal voltage is maintained, the life of your sensitive electronics is extended and they keep working at their best." (source: Tripplite.com)*

Figure 52 - Power Conditioner

Stage lighting – "*Stage lighting is the craft of lighting as it applies to the production of theatre, dance, opera, and other performance arts.*" *(source: Wikipedia.org)*

Figure 53 - Stage Lighting

Headset & In-Ear Monitors – "*In-ear monitors (IEMs) are devices used by musicians, audio engineers, and audiophiles to listen to music or to hear a personal mix of vocals and stage instrumentation for live performance or recording studio mixing. They are often custom fitted for an individual's ears to provide comfort and a high level of noise reduction from ambient surroundings.*" *(source: Wikipedia.org)*

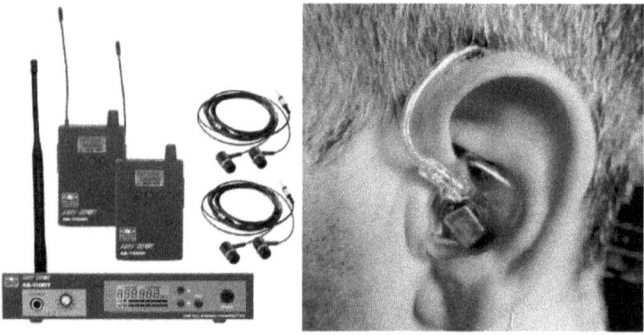

Figure 54 - In-ear Monitor system

Effects Processor – "**Rack-mounted** *effects are typically built in a thin metal chassis with metal "ears" designed to be screwed into a 19-inch rack that is standard to the telecommunication, computing, and music technology industries.*" *(source: Wikipedia.org)*

Figure 55 - Effects Module

Complete Church Sound Systems – This is a typical complete church sound system package that includes everything you need for a service.

Figure 56 - Complete Church Sound System Package

Audio Worship Backing Tracks – Often churches may not have a praise and worship team or a band for services. An alternative to having a live praise and worship team is using instrumental tracks. These tracks allow your congregation to sing to a prerecorded instrumental. The term for this varies from stims, backing tracks, instrumentals, loops, click tracks, midi tracks etc. Since this book is focused on providing the sound and not the actual content I will briefly describe what a backing track is. Let's say you just heard a wonderful inspirational gospel song by one of your favorite gospel artists. If you don't have a praise team or band to perform the song. You can use pre-recorded instrumentals instead or in addition. Sound systems for churches can be elaborate. You can play the video of a song on a projected screen or large video monitor. The video can contain lyrics of the song so the congregation can sing along. These tracks can be played in a software program specially designed for church worship such as Easy Worship, ProPresenter, or MediaShout. Until now I did not list any prices of sound equipment in this book. A sample price for church-specific media software can run up to $399+. (Keep in mind that this is a one-time price). If you hire a full-time band including worship leaders and choir members you could easily pay twice that amount for each service to each musician or choir leader.

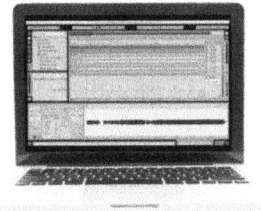

Figure 57 - Laptop

Direct Box (DI box) – *"The DI performs level matching, balancing, and either active buffering or passive impedance matching/impedance bridging to minimize unwanted noise, distortion, and ground loops." (source: Pyleaudio.com)*

Figure 58 - Direct Box

Preferred Brands: Livewire, Behringer, Radial Engineering, Universal Audio, ART, Whirlwind, Pyle Pro

---

Computer Systems – Computer systems allow you to run software related to sound and visual effects for your service. The preferred platform to use is a Mac (Macintosh) because of its ability to run both audio and video. Another alternative is to use a powerful PC (Personal Computer) designed for high-end audio and an accelerated video card. Regardless of which platform you choose to use you must ensure that the processor, memory, and storage are adequate for its use. Computer systems allow you to run presentation software, music for praise and worship, digital mixers, and sound processors such as compressors, effects, and limiters. It is more stable to use a computer for audio than it is to use a standard cd player. A CD may have scratches and can skip during a performance. By using a computer, you can play MP3 or WAV files that will not skip during the service. It is possible to run both Mac and PC for different applications.

Figure 59 – 27" iMac

Figure 60 - PC

The Best Audio Set Up

The best setup for one church is not necessarily the best for another church. The three largest pushbacks that I see that churches use as excuses not to take care of the equipment are: pointing the finger at who is responsible for the upkeep of the equipment, the unwillingness to "change", and the lack of a budget to upgrade the equipment. It's amazing how every department has funds to upgrade but the sound department is neglected and is never considered to be a "real" ministry. Notice that I said sound and not music department. Without the sound department, the music department would not be heard. A church usually will focus on choir robes but they do not focus on the drum snare head that allows the choir to sing on time. The best setup for a church requires three different systems working together as one. These systems can be centralized in one location such as a sound room. You can also have 3 different systems working together. I feel this is the largest problem with church sound systems. They are running 2 or more systems vs. running one. The three components for the best setup are a P.A. system, a musician playback system, and monitoring system.

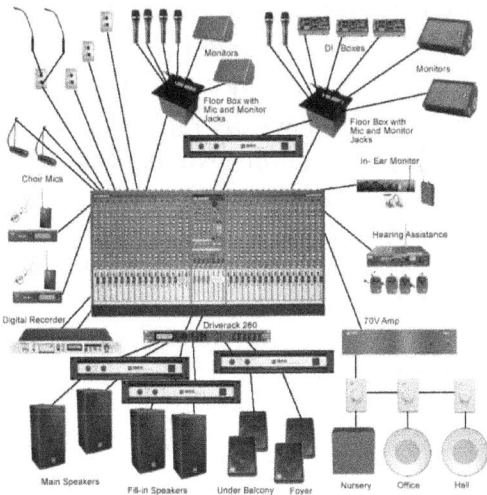

Figure 61 - Complete Sound System

#1 P.A. system – The P.A. system should be controlled by one FOH engineer. Often this person does not exist. The person that can control the FOH is often one of the musicians, several different people, or a music ministry leader (which I feel is a part of the problem). A P.A. system is for the congregation to hear the preacher or singers. Often the same mics that you used to sing through are the same mics that any given preacher would deliver their message with. I feel this should not be the case (but that's another story). The P.A. system can include a wireless or wired mic which is connected to a centralized mixer. A P.A. system should only include voices not music, often music and voices are used by the same speakers. This can cause distortion and the key to equal sound are to have a "clean" sound. If both music and vocals are coming through the same speaker the best thing to do is avoid louder volumes. The music can distort the vocals if the speakers are not dynamic or have high-quality crossovers to separate frequencies. If possible music should be played through a separate loudspeaker system. A shortcut or alternative to avoiding this problem is to play music on one side (left) and play the music on the (right) side. This may not be a practical solution. If you experience voices being muffled or distorted each time the bass of the music hits. You can either reduce the volume or the bass of the music to allow vocals to be heard clearly. In most cases, both music and voice do come out of the same speaker. A P. A. system is usually a set of 2 speakers. A P.A. loudspeaker set is usually located on the left and right sides of the church. Typically, left, and right speaker setup would require a stereo output. Concerning voice in a church using a P.A. system, using a mono setting is appropriate. However, if you play music through the same P.A. system then the music should be set up as stereo output. The P.A. system should be stand-alone and not depend on instruments or even monitors. The P.A. system should always be on and available. At any given time, someone should be able to grab any mic and instantly have the desired volume and EQ. For whatever reason, some of those who work at the church mixer will mute the channel and unmute the channel as needed. The largest issue with this is finding people who will be dependable, alert, and reliable during every service including rehearsals. The point I'm making is often no one is dedicated to sit at the mixer the entire service. So, when someone needs a mic unmuted either the person is not paying attention or not behind the mixer. So, what is the solution? It's simple. Turn on ALL of your mics at the same time. Set the volumes of each mic just before peaking. Then leave the mixer alone. The only issue with this method is acoustics and room density. You may or may not notice a change in the way your mics react or perform inside of an empty church vs. a filled church. Try to set the highest level of each mic channel during a live service. Then leave the mixer alone. No need to mute and unmute mic channels. This is a waste of time and this causes someone to constantly man the mixer at all times.

Figure 62 - P.A. System

#2 Musician Playback – The musician playback could/should be controlled by each musician. The volume of their instrument should satisfy their playback. The musician should not control the playback for the audience in a larger church. The audience playback should be controlled by the FOH. Playback for each musician is determined by several factors. One factor includes which instrument is being used. The other depends on how much control the musician has on adjusting the FOH settings. An organ player has a Leslie which is an external amp/speaker for the organ. The organist should only be concerned about how they hear this when they play. The FOH should have that Leslie mic'ed so that the FOH can adjust the playback for the congregation. You should see the issue with this because the musician is usually responsible for playing for the entire church so they turn up their volume to fill up the entire church. The optimal setup would require that each musician controls their playback with their instrument. A bass and guitar player has their amp. This amp may have enough wattage to be heard by the entire church. However, in professional environments, those amps are connected to the FOH and the FOH adjusts the playback for the audience. The individual guitar and bass amps are then used as stage monitors for that musician and others who may be able to hear it. Placement of the musician's amps are key to getting an equal and "clean" sound. As stated the musician should NOT control the playback for the audience. However, this type of configuration does not apply to a smaller church or venue. How do you know when to use a FOH? This is simple. If the drummer says that they can't hear the singers, if the singers say that they can't hear the piano or keyboard, if the keyboardist says that they can't hear the bass or the guitar... then you need to use a monitoring system which is described below. The problem is that the musicians are cranking their volumes to be heard, using a FOH to provide congregational playback reduces the overall on-stage volume because the musician only needs to adjust their playback. The keyboardist is trying to use their "playback" as both playbacks for themselves AND they are trying to fill up the room. This is the heart of the issue. If the keyboardist turns up their volume it forces other musicians to turn up their volume to compensate. It also forces singers to sing louder if they don't use mics properly. If the keyboardist would control their own volume i.e. Have a speaker next to them and adjust their playback and send their audio to the FOH. Then, the keyboardist can control their own playback for themselves or the stage and the FOH can control the keyboardist volume for the congregation. This type of setup requires "Christians" to work together. What I've experienced is that people DON'T work professionally together and everyone wants to "control" their sound. Many musicians are paid musicians and do not have any spiritual connection to the church. The sound system is not centralized. This is why there are so many audio issues in the church.

#3 Monitoring System – A monitoring system can be located on the pulpit or stage by using a separate special mixer dedicated to distributing the playback for each instrument and the choir to each area/zone. A monitoring system can also be controlled by the FOH mixer by using buses or auxiliary out or sends which is discussed in the section discussing mixers. A monitoring system would require 3 elements. A mixer that has Aux outs or sends, each channel needs a dedicated amp channel and each area needs one monitor (passive or powered). A monitoring system resolves the issue with musicians playing loud just to hear themselves. The monitoring system resolves the issue of musicians not hearing other musicians. The monitoring system resolves the issue with the overall loudness of the pulpit or stage by giving each area or musician their own special mix (playback). This is explained in the Mixer section. Another example of using a monitoring system would be to allow the drummer to have their playback. This would also reduce the need for the drummer to play loud or hard. The problem I've noticed with most churches is lack of communication which is also under Speakers and Monitors. Musicians are not communicating with other musicians either using hand signals or headsets. This is how professionals conduct live performances. I talk more about headsets in the Speakers and Monitors section. The method used for playback can vary. You can use powered amps, passive stage monitors, or in-ear monitors for playback.

Figure 63 - Stage Monitors

Recording the Service

There is always a right and wrong way to do things. The proper way to record a service is to connect the audio out from the mixer/console to the video camera's audio in. That way you will be able to record only the sounds that run through the mixer. This is dependent on you sending all of the audio to the mixer. Which includes all mics, keyboards, organs, drums, guitars, etc. (that is what a mixer is for). The FOH mixer will mix all of the sounds. The output or mix of all of the sounds are then sent to a recording device. You can send the audio to either an audio-only recording device or you can send the signal to a video camera. Many mixers may have a "Tape Out" line (usually RCA). Or it may have multiple main outs. Your mixer may send out a signal that would be sufficient to record the mixed audio signals. Some devices may allow you to make multiple CD copies of a service in one unit. The unit may have 5 to 10 CD bays that will allow you to make multiple copies at once.

Figure 64 - CD Duplicator

My Experience: My issue with recording the service and creating disks at the end of the same service is the fact that the audio is not edited. Whatever was sent to the recording device is the recording you get. If the recording is not being paused and carefully selected your CD you will have one large recording. E.g., If the service was a 90-minute service, you will have a 90-minute long "track" or "song". Meaning the audio would not exclude any unwanted audio. The way to prevent this is to take the raw audio recording home or into a studio and edit down the service into individual parts. E.g., Praise and worship (track 1), Prayer (track 2), Introduction to the speaker (track 3), soloist (track 4), main message (track 6), benediction (track 7), closing prayer (track 8), etc. When all you wanted was the main message or you just wanted to hear the praise and worship service. The problem is that you will not be able to fast forward or skip to the specific section or part of the service since the audio file was not edited.

Preferred Brands: Tascam, Alesis, Akai, Fostex, Korg, Roland, Shure, Sony

Sound Check (the bad word!)

Why do some churches say that they are running the church as a business but they do not run the sound system professionally? In live performances, it is mandatory to have a sound check days, hours, or even minutes before a show. A church service is not a show or entertainment but the equipment involved is the same. A sound check is not just a rehearsal of vocals and instrument levels. A sound check ensures that everything is working correctly. You can place the mic volume levels and EQ, you can make sure there are batteries in the mics and other wireless devices, and you can make sure the loudspeakers and monitors are working correctly and that all equipment and gear are working. I've been attending churches for years (at the time I wrote this book) I have never seen a sound check performed by any church. A sound check can also include cueing playback songs for a vocalist who will use a CD or Mp3 to sing too. Everyone claims to be professional but is not doing what professionals do. A sound check would require extra commitment from the sound team and the musicians which are usually (and sadly) the same people. The sound team should include anything that has to do with playback which includes running the mixer, mics, stands, loudspeaker, cables, church-owned equipment, etc. The sound check ensures that the service will run unhindered.

My Experience: Unfortunately, I don't have a lot of experience with sound checks. People who are set to sing/perform during a service never gives the engineer or musicians a CD until they are about to perform. Why is that? If a professional vocalist or band will perform there will be a mandatory "sound check" before the event. This ensures that the levels are correct, the correct tracks are selected, and the device being used to playback is in proper working order. This includes checking the batteries, using the correct input cables, and knowing how the CD will be played back. Far as live musicians go having a sound check will ensure the proper songs are selected for the performer. Each musician would know which version or key the song will be performed etc. I scratch my head every time I see a vocalist hands, someone, a CD right before they take the mic. I scratch my head every time I see two or more people struggle to get sound from a cell phone or other device without having the proper input cable. I scratch my head when I see engineers struggle to get a CD or audio to play. The main reason is that no one thinks ahead. No one anticipates that there may be a CD, MP3, or any other media that needs to play. No one takes the extra step to prepare for something that may go wrong. This is easily done by dedicating channels specifically for playback with your mixer. You can make sure that whoever is ever on the program to sing bring the audio person a CD or device <u>before</u> service. Why hold up the service because no one is taking the extra step to be professional? A sound check will ensure CDs and MP3s are cued up and will play when needed.

Safety

Cable safety – On a stage or in a church environment you will have an array of audio equipment. Most equipment will require at least two sets of cables which include both power and audio. These cables can run inside walls, ceilings, or floor panels. These cables can cause a tripping hazard for those who are not watching their step. Simply taping cables is not always recommended if cables need to be accessed. Using cable ties such as zip ties and Velcro can help organize cables to prevent clutter and tripping hazards. Cables are very fragile depending on the construction and design of the audio cables. The rule of thumb is to run or hid cables away from a heavily walked area or location. The use of Snake Boxes, wireless systems, and mounting equipment on the ceiling can assist in preventing tripping hazards. There is some caution that should be taken when running non-fireproof wire in the walls or ceiling. Wires have fire ratings and running flammable wires near heat sources such as lights and electrical outlets can cause a fire hazard. I've seen someone run both audio and power cables over lights in the ceiling of a church. If the lights heat up the wire it will ignite. This is cause for the fire marshal to shut the church down.

Figure 65 - Flame Rated Wire

Mounting Speakers – The position of speakers and monitors are essential for getting an equal and distributed sound. Many churches are designed with ceiling or wall-mounted speakers. This type of installation saves space and reduces cable clutter. Mounting speakers can be dangerous if the construction is not sturdy or if the speakers are too heavy for support. Speakers mounted on walls or ceilings must be reinforced with cables and or chains to prevent falling damage due to an earthquake or some other structural incident. Often loudspeakers are mounted on a tripod type of pole. These speaker stands are usually secure and sturdy enough to hold up most P.A. loudspeakers. The downside of the Tripod type of speaker stands is the threat that the speaker can be toppled if the cable or tri-pod legs are tripped over. You must carefully place your speaker stands for both good play back and for safety.

My Experience: I have never seen any issues with speaker mounting or speaker stand causing any damage. The rule of thumb is to run audio cables separate from power cables to avoid interference.

Sound Check Checklist

1. Power On
2. Batteries Charged
3. Mics unmuted
4. All Monitors are working
5. All loudspeakers are on and working
6. Cables won't cause a tripping hazard
7. Mixer levels are marked and set
8. Musicians can hear their desired playback
9. FOH has an even mix
10. Songs for the service are cued up and ready to play
11. The sound engineer has a copy of the program

Church Sound Ministry Quiz

Multiple Choice.

Identify the choice that best completes the statement or answers the question.

1. **What is the benefit of having a control room?**
   A. A private place to talk during the service
   B. A place you can store personal items
   C. Centralized Control over the sound
   D. A convenient place to keep unwanted tools and equipment

2. **What can help improve the sound before a service?**
   A. Sound Check
   B. Re-wire entire system
   C. Turn off all of the mic's
   D. Disconnect all monitors

3. **What is the Best way to record audio for a service?**
   A. Move audio recording device closer to the speakers
   B. Connect camera audio input to the mixer audio output
   C. Use a cellphone to record the audio
   D. Use a tablet to record the audio

4. **How many channels does a typical Stereo (left and right) amp has?**
   A. 4
   B. 1
   C. 2
   D. None

5. **What is not a part of a typical P.A. System?**
   A. Microphone
   B. Amp
   C. Speakers
   D. Compressor
   E. Cables
   F. Speaker Stands

6. **Which type of microphone is commonly used on stage?**
   A. Shotgun
   B. Cardiod
   C. Directional
   D. Dynamic

7. **What type of audio connection should be used if you do not have 1/4-inch instrument cables?**

A. RCA
B. USB
C. XLR
D. PS3

8. **Which is not a purpose of using a drum cage or drum shield?**
   A. Allow drummer to play as loud as they want
   B. Focus drum sound to a specific direction
   C. Isolating the drums from a specific immediate area
   D. Recording the drums

9. **Before mic's used XLR connectors which connector was used?**
   A. PS2 connector
   B. USB
   C. 1/4-inch phone connector (instrument cable)
   D. Firewire

10. **Having more amps allows you to have more?**
    A. Lights
    B. Mixers
    C. Monitors and Loudspeakers
    D. Effects

11. **Which devices can be used to play music during a service?**
    A. CD player
    B. MP3 player
    C. Cell Phone
    D. Tablet
    E. iPhone
    F. Laptop
    G. All of the Above

12. **What is a passive monitor or speaker?**
    A. A monitor or speaker that has power
    B. A monitor that has a built-in EQ
    C. An amp that has 4 channels
    D. A monitor or speaker that is not powered

13. **What is a physical trait to identify a monitor vs. a loudspeaker?**
    A. Triangular Shaped speaker
    B. Round shaped speaker
    C. Wedge shaped speaker
    D. Square shaped speaker

14. **What is the benefit of using a digital mixer?**
    A. Save and recall user settings
    B. Compact size

C. Multiple channels and busses
D. Cleaner audio signal
E. All of the Above
F. None of the Above

15. **Which components are required for the best professional set up?**
    A. P.A. System for voice and music
    B. Musicians only control their own playback
    C. FOH control Monitors for musicians and stage playback
    D. All of the Above

How do you get started?

Do you want to design or improve your sound system?

The first important questions to consider when designing or upgrading your sound system are what exactly do you want? What is your budget? And what equipment do you currently have?

What do you want?

_____

What is your budget for your sound system?

_____

Check one of the following packages:

_____

Package A – You have a **"large budget"** set aside for design or upgrading. You have at least $2,000+ for designing or upgrading your sound system. You will pay for exactly what you need for a professional sound system.

_____

Package B – You will only purchase **"as-needed"** equipment. You will purchase some equipment but on a smaller budget not to exceed $1,000. This will ensure that cables and connectors are updated. You may only need to purchase a few pieces of equipment, not a full system.

_____

Package C – You have **"no budget"** to upgrade or to make additional purchases. You need to work with the existing equipment that you have. This will optimize your current equipment to the best of its performance. You have no money to make any additional purchases including equipment that you may need. We will work with what you currently have to enhance the sound of your system.

List Your Current Equipment

Mixer Brand _____ How many Aux/Busses/Subs/Sends ____

Mixer Connector Type(s):   XLR ____   ¼" ____   RCA ____   Speakon ____

P.A. System _____

P.A. Connector Type(s):   XLR ____   ¼" ____   RCA ____   Speakon ____

Amp _____

Loudspeakers _____

Monitors _____

Wireless Microphone(s): _____

Wired Microphone(s): _____

CD Player _____

Other Audio Input Device _____

Stage Snake connector type _____   Amount of inputs/outputs

List Equipment Needed

Mixer ____

Mixer Connector Type(s):   XLR ____   ¼" ____   RCA ____   Speakon ____

P.A. System ____

P.A. Connector Type(s):   XLR ____   ¼" ____   RCA ____   Speakon ____

Amp ____

Loudspeakers ____

Monitors ____

Wireless Microphone(s): ____

Wired Microphone(s): ____

CD Player ____

Other Audio Input Device ____

Stage Snake connector type ____   Number of inputs/outputs ____

Typical Complete P.A. System

1. 8-16 Channel Mixer w/ 4+ busses
2. Amp (1000watt) – 2-4 channel
3. Loudspeaker x2 - Active
4. Loudspeaker stands
5. Monitors x2 (wedges) - Passive
6. Wireless Microphones x 3/4
7. Microphone stands
8. Cables: XLR, 1/4" Instrument Cables, ¼" Patch cables
9. Connectors and Adapters: Speakon, ¼" to XLR
10. Rechargeable Batteries
11. Snake/Stage Box

Quiz Answers

Question 1.   ANS: C

Question 2.   ANS: A

Question 3.   ANS: B

Question 4.   ANS: C

Question 5.   ANS: D

Question 6.   ANS: D

Question 7.   ANS: C

Question 8.   ANS: A

Question 9.   ANS: C

Question 10. ANS: C

Question 11. ANS: G

Question 12. ANS: D

Question 13. ANS: C

Question 14. ANS: E

Question 15. ANS: D

Index of Figures

Figure 1 - Mixer Setup 9
Figure 2 - Analog Mixer 10
Figure 3 - Digital Mixer 11
Figure 4 – Rack Mountable Digital Mixer With Software 11
Figure 5 - Powered Mixer 11
Figure 6 - Typical P.A. System 12
Figure 7 - Mixing Console 12
Figure 8 - Mackie 24x8 8-Bus Series Mixing Console 13
Figure 9 - Mixer with Auxiliary Outs 14
Figure 10 - A 4 channel (non-auxiliary) mixers I own 14
Figure 11 - Mixer Aux Channels 15
Figure 12 - EQ 15
Figure 13 - VU Meter 16
Figure 14 - Sanctuary 16
Figure 15 - Acoustical Wall Panels to absorb sound 17
Figure 16 - 4 Channel Amplifier 19
Figure 17 - P.A. System 20
Figure 18 - Loud Speaker 21
Figure 19 - On Stage Monitor 21
Figure 20 - Ceiling Monitor 23
Figure 21 - Wireless Speaker System 23
Figure 22 - Guitar Amp 24
Figure 23 - Bass Amp 24
Figure 24 – Headset 25
Figure 25 - XLR 25
Figure 26 - 2x ¼" Male and 1x Female (mono) 26
Figure 27 - 3.5mm Mini Phone Connector 26
Figure 28 - Speakon connector 26
Figure 29 - RCA 26
Figure 30 - Snake Box 27
Figure 31 - Attenuation 27
Figure 32 - Audio Repeater 27
Figure 33 - Dynamic Microphone 28
Figure 34 - Shotgun Microphone 29
Figure 35 - XLR 29
Figure 36 - Wireless Microphone System 30
Figure 37 - Cheap mic using a phono jack 30
Figure 38 - Rechargeable Batteries 31
Figure 39 - Typical Microphone Stand 31
Figure 40 - Rear of Mixer 32
Figure 41 - CD player 32
Figure 42 - Typical Drum Cage 33
Figure 43 - Drum Room 33
Figure 44 - Drum Seat Amplifier 34
Figure 45 - Compressor 36
Figure 46 - Noise Gate 36

Figure 47 - Limiter 36
Figure 48 - Equalizer 36
Figure 49 - Cabinet 37
Figure 50 - Power Strip 37
Figure 51 - Surge Protector 37
Figure 52 - Power Conditioner...38
Figure 53 - Stage Lighting...38
Figure 54 - In-ear Monitor system...38
Figure 55 - Effects Module 38
Figure 56 - Complete Church Sound System Package..39
Figure 57 - Laptop..39
Figure 58 - Direct Box 40
Figure 59 – 27" iMac 40
Figure 60 - PC...40
Figure 61 - Complete Sound System 41
Figure 62 - P.A. System 42
Figure 63 - Stage Monitors..44
Figure 64 - CD Duplicator 44
Figure 65 - Flame Rated Wire...46

Draw a diagram of your church sound system

www.ingramcontent.com/pod-product-compliance
Lightning Source LLC
LaVergne TN
LVHW061316060426
835507LV00019B/2186